The Chocolate Connection

Jillian Powell

Contents

OXFORD
UNIVERSITY PRESS

The best job in the world?

Mmmm, marvellous, mouthwatering chocolate ... if only it grew on trees.

Luckily for the world's chocolate fans, it does! Chocolate bars, hot chocolate and even chocolate ice-cream are all made from the seeds (beans) of **cacao** (ka-kay-oh) trees.

However, you won't find chocolate trees in your local park. They mainly grow in Central and South America. Before you beg your parents to move there, you should know something. The raw beans taste disgusting. It's hard work turning them into delicious chocolate ... later we'll meet some of the people whose job it is to help!

A cacao tree produces 20–30 pods full of beans every year.

An historical illustration of cocoa beans.

Chocolate firsts

Do you remember the first time you tasted chocolate? Check out these other firsts in chocolate's long history.

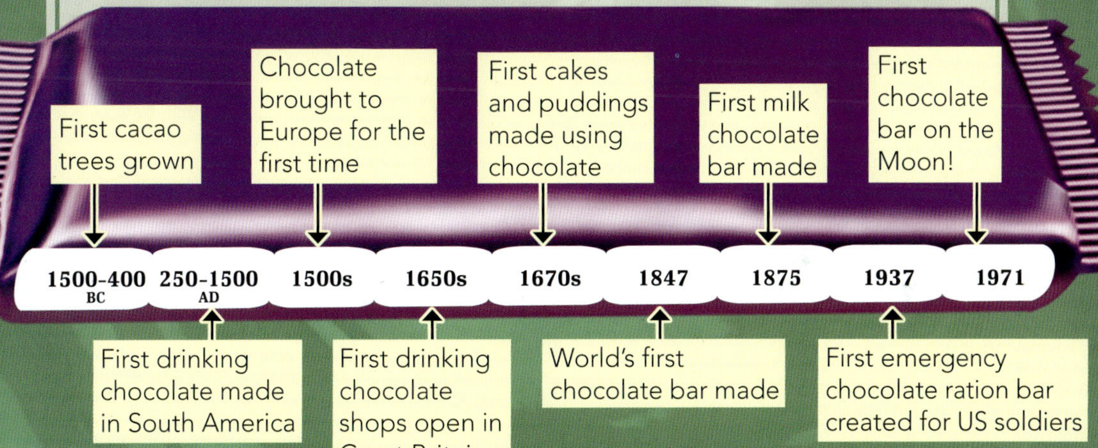

Gruesome history

Chocolate's journey from the seed on the cacao tree to the delicious treat we love today started thousands of years ago. It's a story of bloodthirsty emperors, thieving sailors, crafty chemists and brilliant inventors. Read on, and you'll realize we're lucky to have chocolate at all!

The bloodthirsty emperor

You've probably heard of hot chocolate but what about cold chocolate? Thousands of years ago, Central American civilizations thought frothy cold chocolate was the best drink ever. They called it **chocolatl** (say: chocolate). The **Maya** and **Aztecs** used it as an energy drink and even a medicine!

The emperor's new drink

Spicy chocolatl was the favourite drink of Aztec nobles, priests, warriors and merchants. To make chocolatl, first the Aztecs roasted cacao beans in clay pots. Next, they ground them, and mixed them with water, vanilla and chilli. Then they whipped the drink or poured it from pot to pot to make frothy foam.

Aztecs making chocolate from cacao beans.

Sound nice? One of the first Europeans to drink chocolatl described it as 'a bitter drink'.

Montezuma II was a cruel Aztec emperor. He ruled over the great Aztec Empire from 1502–1520. He was famous for drinking chocolate mixed with the blood of **rebels** – yuck! Montezuma's victims didn't have much to thank him for … but you do! He introduced chocolate to the Spanish explorers. They brought chocolate back to Europe (without Montezuma's gruesome added ingredient, of course).

Quetzalcoatl (say: kwet-sil-co-art-il) was known as the 'chocolate god'. The Aztecs believed he gave them the gift of cacao.

Montezuma loved chocolate so much, he drank fifty cups a day!

Chocolate challenge!

Make Aztec chocolate

Add cinnamon, vanilla or nutmeg to your hot chocolate. Let it cool, then whisk it to make it frothy. Add ice cubes to make it extra cold!

The cunning explorer

Hernán Cortés was a Spanish soldier and explorer. In 1517, he landed on the Mexican coast with 11 ships and 600 sailors (he didn't believe in packing lightly!). Cortés was hunting for Aztec treasures to take home to Spain. Our old friend Montezuma welcomed him with glittering gifts. He also served up a lavish feast including something even better than gold ... drinking chocolate!

Cortés receiving gifts from the Aztec emperor Montezuma on his arrival in Mexico.

A sticky end

Poor Montezuma found out the Spanish were only after his treasures. He was taken captive by Cortés' men and killed in 1520.

Chocolate money

What would your local shopkeeper say if you tried to pay them in chocolate? Cortés learned that cacao beans were so prized by the Aztecs they were used as money. He hatched a cunning plan to set up cacao plantations and grow this 'money' for Spain!

Money you can eat!

True or false?

Cortés was the first European to discover chocolate.

False: Christopher Columbus captured a cargo of cacao beans on his last voyage to the Americas in 1502. One report says he presented chocolate to the Spanish king and queen, but they hated the bitter taste.

Chocolate soldiers

Cortés began giving chocolatl to his soldiers to give them strength and energy. He claimed they could march all day after drinking just one cup! In 1528, Cortés returned from Mexico to Spain with cacao beans and tools for grinding and whipping (the chocolate, not the soldiers!).

Cortés wrote home to King Charles V of Spain, telling him about chocolate.

... a divine drink, which builds up resistance and fights fatigue ...

Cortés arriving in Tlaxcala (say: tla-sca-la) after his victory at Otumba.

A spoonful of sugar...

Soldiers were tough enough to drink cold, bitter chocolatl ... but was it a drink that everyone would like? Spanish monks started adding sugar, honey and vanilla, and served the drink steaming hot. Spain's secret recipe was kept for nearly 100 years before the rest of Europe caught on.

The Spanish sailors were not happy to see their precious cargo thrown overboard!

Chocolate houses

Imagine being born in the era BCC (Before Chocolate Cake). Disaster! Luckily, chocolate took Europe by storm in the 1600s. Other countries set up plantations and began shipping cacao beans from the Americas.

Cooks began to use ground cacao to make rich puddings and chocolate rolls. In 1662, **Hannah Woolley** wrote this recipe in one of the world's first cookery books.

Recipe for Spanish Chaculata

1. Boil some water in an earthen pipkin (small pot) a quarter of an hour.

2. Sweeten it with sugar.

3. Scrape your chaculata [chocolate] very fine.

4. Put it in and boil half an hour.

5. Add the yolks of eggs well beaten.

6. Stir over a slow fire til it be thick.

Brilliant – HOUSES made of chocolate!

It wasn't long before chocolate houses began to appear on the streets. They weren't houses made of chocolate though! They were cafés where rich people could drink hot chocolate! The most famous was White's, which opened in London in 1693. The owner, **Francesco White**, kept his customers entertained by doing magic tricks and playing the fiddle.

True or false?

King Charles II tried to shut down all chocolate and coffee houses.

True: They were seen as places where rebels could hatch plots against the king and where lazy workmen wasted time!

300 years ago, hot chocolate was a drink for rich people.

Chocolate doctors

The discovery of chocolate excited 17th-century doctors, too. It was promoted as a health food that could cure everything from bad breath to bad backs!

While working in Jamaica, English doctor **Henry Stubbe** researched the effects of chocolate. In 1662, he wrote a book called *The Indian Nectar*. He was full of praise for its use in medicine. He claimed that chocolate could give you energy, help with digestion and depression, and even make your heart stronger.

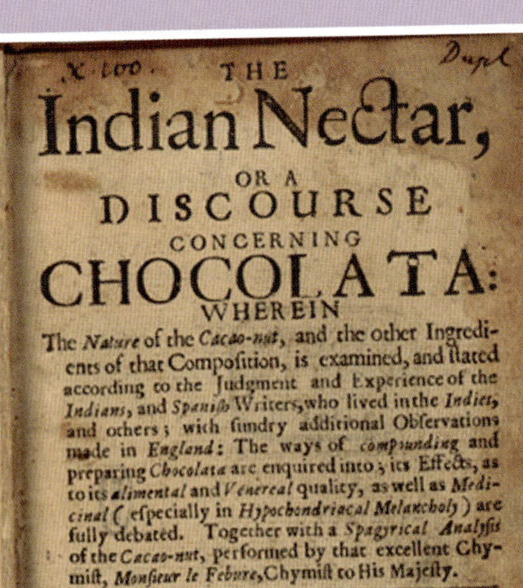

THE

Indian Nectar,

OR A

DISCOURSE

CONCERNING

CHOCOLATA:

WHEREIN

The *Nature* of the *Cacao-nut*, and the other Ingredients of that Composition, is examined, and stated according to the Judgment and Experience of the *Indians*, and *Spanish* Writers, who lived in the *Indies*, and others; with sundry additional Observations made in *England*: The ways of *compounding* and preparing *Chocolata* are enquired into; its Effects, as to its *alimental* and *Venereal* quality, as well as *Medicinal* (especially in *Hypochondriacal Melancholy*) are fully debated. Together with a *Spagyrical Analysis* of the *Cacao-nut*, performed by that excellent Chymist, *Monsieur le Febure*, Chymist to His Majesty.

By Henry Stubbe *formerly of* Ch. Ch. *in* Oxon. *Physician for His Majesty, and the Right Honourable* Thomas Lord Windsor *in the Island of* Jamaica *in the* West-Indies.

Thomas Gage, Survey of the *West-Indies.* chap. 15. Here in a certain part of *Guaxaca*) grow many Trees of Cacao, and Achiote, *whereof is made the* Chocolatte, *and is a Commodity of much trading in those parts, though our* English *and* Hollanders *make little use of it, when they take a prize at Sea, or not knowing the secret virtue and quality of it for the good of the* Stomach. ——— *Videant, intabescántque relictâ.*

London, Printed by *J.C.* for *Andrew Crook* at the Sign of the Great Dragon in St. *Paul's* Church-yard. 1662.

An extract from Henry Stubbe's book *The Indian Nectar*.

True or false?

Chilli-flavoured chocolate is a 21st-century novelty.

False! Henry Stubbe wrote chocolate recipes that used chilli. In fact, the combination goes right back to the Maya and Aztecs, who added chillies to their chocolatl.

A spoonful of cocoa helps the medicine go down

When French Queen Marie Antoinette complained that her medicine tasted revolting. Her royal chemist, **Sulpice Debauve**, sprung into action. In the 1790s, he disguised her medicine in little round chocolates. He called these medicine chocolates 'pistoles'. They became so popular that Debauve went on to open chocolate shops throughout France. Debauve worked with his nephew, Antoine Gallais. They sold 'healthy chocolates' tasting of almond milk, vanilla and orange-blossom water.

Debauve moved from chemist to chocolatier!

Debauve's *pistoles* are still sold today but without the medicine!

Unfortunately, today's doctors know chocolate is NOT a medicine. The next best thing? Medicine that tastes like chocolate! Maybe if you were a king or queen ...

True or False?

Chocolate making is a science.

True! Many early chocolate makers were chemists. They had the skills and tools to grind and blend ingredients.

Problem solvers

Fancy a bite of 350-year-old chocolate? Be careful – the cacao cakes and puddings made in the 1670s were nowhere near as nice as today's chocolate.

The problem was that the fat in cacao beans – known as cocoa butter – made them hard to **process**. Ground cacao had to be boiled for a long time, or whipped up with egg yolks and milk to help the fats dissolve.

It would take a long time to make just one cake!

Chocolate factories

English chemist Joseph Fry began making drinking chocolate in 1759. His son, **Joseph Storrs Fry**, took over the business in 1795. He brought in the latest steam-powered machinery to grind the cacao beans. Factory-made chocolate was born!

The machines could work faster, grind more beans and produce finer cocoa powder than hand grinders. J.S. Fry & Sons soon became the biggest chocolate factory in Britain.

Hooray for the Industrial Revolution – new machinery meant more chocolate and it was cheaper too!

The production line in a modern chocolate factory.

The cocoa press

Meet **Casparus van Houten** – the man who changed the world (well, the chocolate industry) forever. In 1828, van Houten invented a machine that squeezed the cocoa butter out of cacao beans.

This made it much easier to grind the beans into a paste. The paste could then be mixed with sugar and just the right amount of cocoa butter to make solid chocolate.

Van Houten's son **Conrad** was just as brilliant as his dad and found a way to break cacao beans down to make a fine powder. This led to the ultimate breakthrough …

Casparus van Houten's cocoa press.

An early poster advertising Cacao van Houten.

... The world's first chocolate bar!

In 1847, Fry's mixed together cocoa powder, sugar and melted cocoa butter to make a gorgeous, gooey mixture that could be shaped into blocks and bars. *Eureka!*

An early 20th-century poster advertising Fry's chocolate.

True or false?

Chocolate can be made using potatoes.

True! Before the cocoa press was invented, cacao was mixed with potato **starch** to help dissolve the cocoa butter.

A chocolate empire

Cadbury's is a world famous chocolate brand. It started as a single shop in Birmingham, selling drinking chocolate, tea and coffee. The owner, **John Cadbury**, ground his own cacao beans by hand.

Cadbury's business did very well. John Cadbury was able to buy a factory and a warehouse. He soon offered customers 11 types of cocoa and 16 types of drinking chocolate!

The chocolate village

John's sons **Richard** and **George** took over Cadbury in 1861. They bought land outside Birmingham to build a new factory and a village for the workers. They wanted to look after their staff and improve their lives.

Cadbury's chocolate village was named Bourneville, after a stream that ran through the site. Sadly, the stream was not full of chocolate milkshake!

Cheaper chocolate

In the 1850s, the law changed. The tax on cacao beans was reduced. Factories could make cheaper chocolate and more people could afford to buy it. Hundreds of different chocolate products were invented and chocolate became big business.

In the 1860s, the Cadbury brothers started using a cocoa press, which meant Cadbury could make 'pure chocolate' without adding starch. By 1899, Cadbury had become one of the most famous chocolate brands in the world.

A 19th-century poster advertising some of Cadbury's chocolate products.

Workers making chocolate eggs at Cadbury's factory in the 1920s.

The military hero

What's the best thing about chocolate? The taste? The way it melts in your mouth? Not true for the US army Ration D bar! The Ration D Bar tasted 'just a little better than a boiled potato'.

U. S. ARMY FIELD RATION D

To be eaten slowly (in about a half hour). Can be dissolved by crumbling into a cup of boiling water, if desired as a beverage.

CONTENTS:
Chocolate, Sugar, Skim Milk Powder, Cocoa Butter, Oat Flour, Vanillin (artificial), B_1 (Thiamin Hydrochloride) 190 I. U.

4 OUNCES NET - 600 CALORIES

Up to 24 million Ration D bars were made every week during World War II.

In 1937, the US Army asked the Hershey Chocolate Corporation to make non-melting chocolate that tasted awful! They wanted bars that soldiers would save until they were starving, rather than chomp as soon as they were given it.

No pockets full of sticky chocolate – Ration D Bars didn't melt!

Energy bars

Hershey's chief chemist **Sam Hinkle** began to experiment. Cutting back on sugar and adding oat flour made the chocolate less tempting. Vitamin B1 was added to keep soldiers healthy. Most importantly, Hinkle's chocolate was packed with energy. Three bars could feed a soldier for a day! Ration D chocolate was a huge success and Hinkle went on to run Hershey.

Sam Hinkle inspects products on the Hershey Chocolate Corporation production line.

True or false?

Chocolate helped to win a war.

True! Hershey won five military awards for 'backing up soldiers on the fighting fronts'.

Real-life Willy Wonkas

Willy Wonka is the world's most famous chocolate maker. In Roald Dahl's story *Charlie and the Chocolate Factory*, Wonka runs a mysterious factory where he invents belly-boggling bars.

Wonka is not real – but some lucky people really do invent chocolates for a living. Next time someone asks what you'd like to do when you grow up, try saying **'chocolatier'**!

Willy Wonka, played by Jonny Depp, and guests in his chocolate factory in the film version of Roald Dahl's book.

True or false?

Chocolate bars are mainly made from … chocolate.

False! Have you ever read a chocolate bar label? (Buy a bar for 'research'!) The 'cacao' or 'cocoa solids' are the chocolate part. Some bars contain 80% or more cocoa solids, but many have 25% or less. Many chocolate bars are made mainly from milk and sugar.

Willie Harcourt-Cooze bought a farm in Venezuela, in South America. He planted 50 000 cacao trees. He wanted to grow rare cacao beans with a brilliant flavour. Back in the UK, he set up a factory. He wanted to make chocolate from just the cacao bean, with no added ingredients. Willie's 100% pure chocolate was invented. It is often used in savoury dishes – exactly how the Maya and Aztecs once used it!

How far would you go to make the perfect chocolate?

Louis has invented more than 1800 chocolate recipes. He loves using weird ingredients, from cola fizz to black pepper, and even meat!

Louis Barnett began making chocolate when he was just eight years old. At first his hobby just made his friends happy – and his family kitchen messy. Then Louis' grandfather lent him money to buy a chocolate-making machine and Louis started a chocolate business. As a teenager, Louis became the youngest person ever to supply supermarkets with chocolate!

Chocolate Challenge!

Be a chocolatier!

Can you invent a weird, wonderful or wacky chocolate recipe? Try tasting chocolate with different foods to find the most tasty combination!

The chocolate taster

It's hard to think of a better job than chocolate maker, except perhaps ... chocolate taster! Do you have what it takes to check that chocolate looks, smells, tastes and feels amazing?

It looks good, it smells good – does it taste good?

Chocolate Challenge!

Which of your friends is the best chocolate taster? Take it in turns to wear a blindfold and taste small pieces of five different chocolate bars. (Explain that you need to buy five chocolate bars in the name of science!) Rank the bars for sweetness, cocoa flavour and special ingredients. Look at the packaging to see who got it right!

My friends ...

- Who has the best sense of smell?
- Who has the most sensitive taste buds?
- Who is the best judge of brands?
- Who loves chocolate the most?

Chloe Doutre-Roussel taught herself to be a chocolate taster when she was a child. She learned to tell different bars apart by tasting them while blindfolded. She now works as chocolate **consultant**, running tasting classes and chocolate tours from her own chocolate shop in Paris, and travelling around the world to meet chocolatiers.

Chloe buys cacao beans from a co-operative of organic Fairtrade growers in Bolivia.

The cacao grower

What would the Aztecs think of high-tech chocolate factories? Today, machines make most of the world's chocolate. However, the journey still starts with tiny cacao beans growing on a tree. Without the world's 6.5 million cacao growers, we would have no chocolate!

Cacao farming is hard work. The cacao pods have to be harvested by hand.

True or false?

Chocolate provides work for millions of people around the world.

True! Around 45 million people rely on chocolate for their income.

Cacao trees grow best in tropical rainforests, but they are also planted on farms in tropical areas of the world.

Comfort Kumeah has a 20-acre farm in Ghana, West Africa. Every day Comfort gets up at 5.30am and walks to her farm where she plants, waters and weeds her crops. The busiest time on the farm is the cacao harvest between September and February. The beans are picked from the tall trees, then **fermented** and dried for several days before they can be sold.

Fair and square

Comfort belongs to a **Fairtrade co-operative** of cacao growers. The Fairtrade organization helps cacao growers get a fair price for their beans. Fairtrade also gives them extra money. This can be used to help farmers and local people. It pays for water wells, schools and community.

The Fairtrade logo

The bug watcher

STOP PRESS! The world has run out of chocolate! Sounds like a nightmare? Some scientists think the world's cacao crops could die off in the next 50 years if we don't take action now. Look at the threats faced by cacao trees:

Insect pests such as cocoa **mirids** and the Cocoa Moth feed on the trees.

Climate change means that parts of the world, such as West Africa, may become too hot to grow cacao.

Fungi such as Frosty Pod Rot cause diseases.

Chocolate heroes!

Scientists are working to understand cacao trees better, to make sure that the future is chocolatey.

Allen Young is a biologist. He spends his days looking at tiny insects called midges – and not just for fun. These insects **pollinate** cacao trees, just like bees pollinate many other plants. Allen looks for ways to get the midges to pollinate more flowers. Bribes don't work – not even free chocolate! However, the midges do their job better on small farms (where cacao grows in the shade of other crops) than on big plantations where cacao is the only crop.

Only a tiny proportion of cacao flowers become pods full of cacao beans.

Chocolate by numbers

Next time you chomp on a chocolate bar, spare a thought for all the people who help bring cocoa from the cacao tree to your lips.

Here are some more chocolate facts to **muse** on as you munch!

20-40
The number of cacao beans inside each pod

6
The number of steps needed to prepare cacao beans for chocolate making (fermentation, drying, cracking, roasting, grinding, pressing)

450 grams
The amount of chocolate that can be made with all the beans grown on this tree in a year

75%
The share of the world's cacao produced in Africa

3
The types of cocoa (Forastero, Criollo, Trinitario)

4
The number of cacao beans that would buy you a rabbit in Aztec times

3 billion
The number of chocolate bars made for soldiers during World War II by American company Hershey